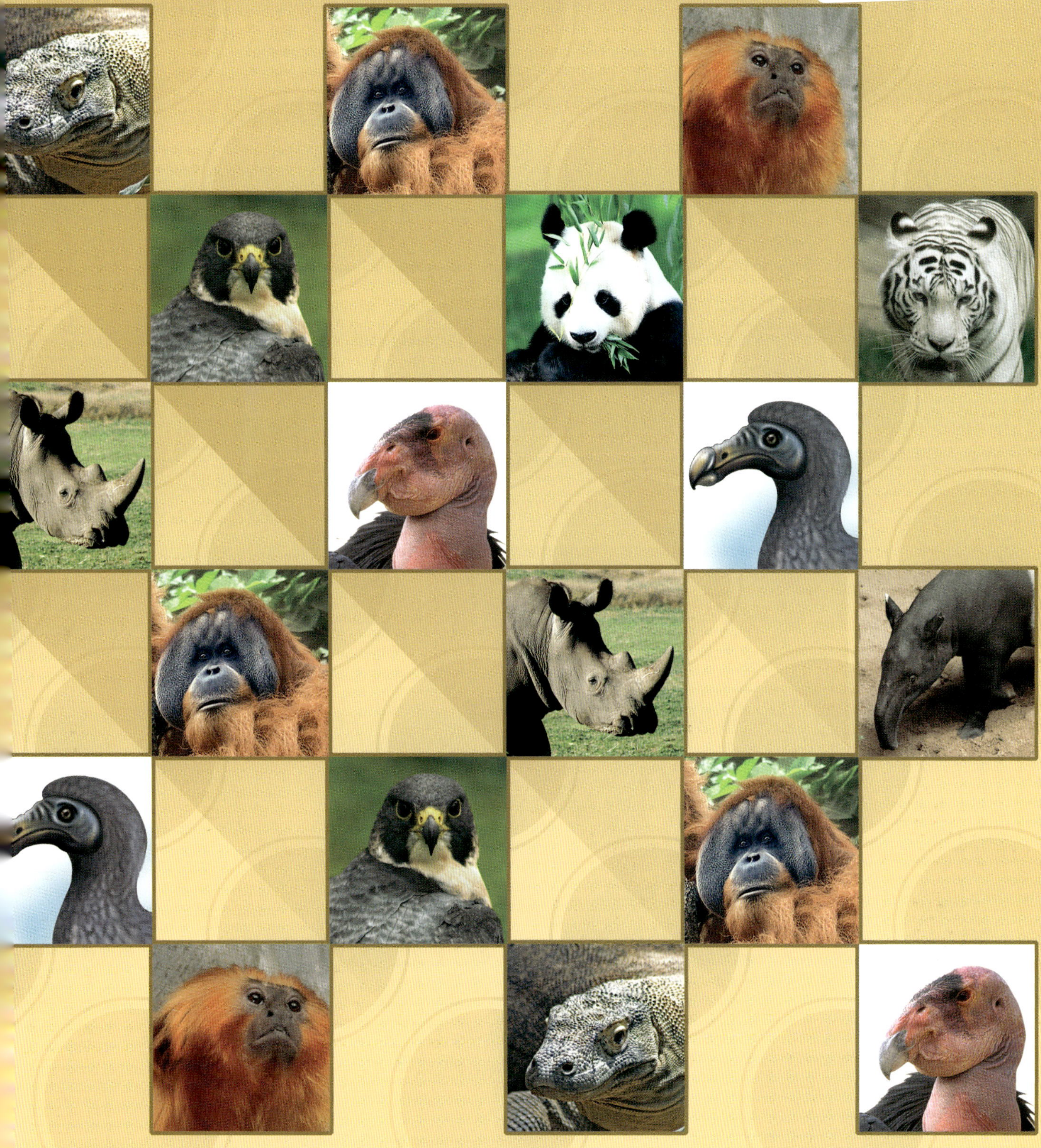

Picture credits:
T=top; B=bottom; C=centre; R=right; L=left

8L Ferenc Cegledi/shutterstock; 9R Peter Doomen/shutterstock; 10R David Hyde/shutterstock;
12T Steven Ciccarelli/shutterstock; 13L Vishal Shah/shutterstock; 14R Vladimir Pomortzeff/shutterstock;
16R Andre Maritz/shutterstock; 16-17C Anita/shutterstock; 17R Kurt De Bruyn/shutterstock;
18B Rui Manuel Teles Gomes/shutterstock; 19R Lynsey Allan/shutterstock;
22R Adrian T Jones/shutterstock; 22L Cindy Haggerty/shutterstock; 25T Jason Stitt/shutterstock;
28T Nathan Holland/shutterstock; 30T N Joy Neish/shutterstock; 30B Stanislav Khrapov/shutterstock;
31R Welland Lau/shutterstock; 34L U.S. Fish and Wildlife Service;
34-35C National Oceanic & Atmospheric Administration (NOAA),U.S. Department of Commerce;
35TR National Oceanic & Atmospheric Administration (NOAA), U.S. Department of Commerce;
35C National Oceanic & Atmospheric Administration (NOAA), U.S. Department of Commerce;
38L Freeze | Dreamstime.com; 38LB U.S. Fish and Wildlife Service;
38-39C Wayne Johnson/shutterstock; 40L Gila R. Todd/shutterstock;
42C kai hecker/shutterstock; base across book-Exxon Valdez Oil Spill Trustee Council;
illustrations by Q2A Media.

Copyright © 2015 North Parade Publishing Ltd.
4-5 North Parade, Bath, England. BA1 1LF
www.nppbooks.co.uk

American Edition Editor
Sean Kennelly

First published: 2006
All rights reserved. No part of this publication may be reported,
stored in a retrieval system or transmitted, in any form or by any means,
electronic, mechanical, photocopying, recording, or otherwise, without
the prior permission of the copyright holder.

Endangered Animals
Contents

Living on the Edge	6
Making the List	8
Apes in Danger	10
Monkey Mania	12
Cats Endangered	14
Crocodilians	16
Other Reptilians	18
Endangering the Elephant	20
Feathered Friends	22
Flightless Birds in Danger	24
Bears on the Brink	26
Endangered Antelopes	28
Rhinos on the Run	30
Canines in Danger	32
Whales on the Edge	34
Sharks Endangered	36
Seals and Sea Cows	38
Saving the Rodents	40
Amphibian Alert	42
Glossary	44
Index	45

LIVING ON THE EDGE

Imagine if you woke up one day to find there were no more elephants left in the world! This is not sensationalism – our world really is at risk! Once, there were dinosaurs on this planet, but today they do not exist anymore. When a particular animal is wiped off the face of the Earth forever, it is said to be extinct. An endangered animal can be defined as one that is in danger of becoming extinct. There are several factors that can bring about such an alarming situation.

MAN – THE BIGGEST ENEMY

In today's world, humans are mainly responsible for animals becoming extinct or endangered. Animals are killed not only for their meat, but also for their skin, teeth, horns and claws. People use them to make jewelery and expensive leather and fur coats. Some people even kill animals for sport. They collect animal horns and skin as trophies, and display them at their homes. Humans are also destroying the homes of animals by cutting down trees and polluting the rivers and seas with poisonous chemicals.

HOSTILE CLIMATE

Sudden changes in the climate caused by global warming can also lead to extinction. Global warming is the rise in the temperature of the planet, caused by an increase in the amount of greenhouse gases – like carbon dioxide – in the atmosphere. These gases trap the Sun's heat, keeping the Earth warm at night. However, when they are present in the atmosphere in large amounts, more heat is trapped making the Earth warmer. Global warming causes the melting of glaciers, heavy rainfalls, extreme drought, floods and fire. Many animals are killed by such extreme climate.

Global warming has led to the melting of large amounts of ice in the polar regions

ALIEN INVASION!

Some species are not naturally found in a particular place. When these species are introduced into that place, they can destroy the existing animals. This is best illustrated by the case of the dodo, a flightless bird of Mauritius that is now extinct. Before humans came to Mauritius, there were hardly any animals on the island that hunted the dodo. Since it had no predators to escape from, scientists conclude the dodo never flew and slowly its wings became weak. When humans arrived at the island, they brought with them animals like dogs, cats, rats and monkeys. These animals, along with humans, hunted the flightless dodo into extinction.

◤ The destruction of the forests by human settlers made the dodo vulnerable, since there was no place for the bird to hide from its new predators

◤ Every animal plays an important role in maintaining the ecological balance of the planet. The extinction of even one of them can greatly upset this balance

FACT FILE
Number of Threatened Species according to the IUCN Red List

Group	2003	2004	2006
Vertebrates			
Mammals	1,130	1,101	1093
Birds	1,194	1,213	1206
Reptiles	293	304	341
Fish	750	800	1173
Amphibians	157	1,770	1811
Invertebrates			
Insects	553	559	623
Molluscs	967	974	975
Crustaceans	409	429	459
Others	30	30	44

ALARMING EFFECTS

The effects of endangering the existence of animals are many and dangerous. When any animal is endangered, it upsets the balance of life on the planet. For example: lions are important in maintaining the balance of wildlife in the grasslands. They feed on plant-eating animals like antelopes and zebras. If lions were wiped out, the population of plant-eating animals would increase alarmingly. This would then lead to the destruction of more plants, and soon there would not be enough plants to feed the animals or to provide shade and oxygen.

Making the List

There are several organizations and programs that monitor the status of animals and plants across the world. These organisations include the International Union for the Conservation of Nature and Natural Resources (IUCN), the Endangered Species Act (ESA) and the Convention on International Trade in Endangered Species of Wild Fauna and Flora (CITES). Each of these organizations has specific laws regarding the listing of endangered species and related conservation programs.

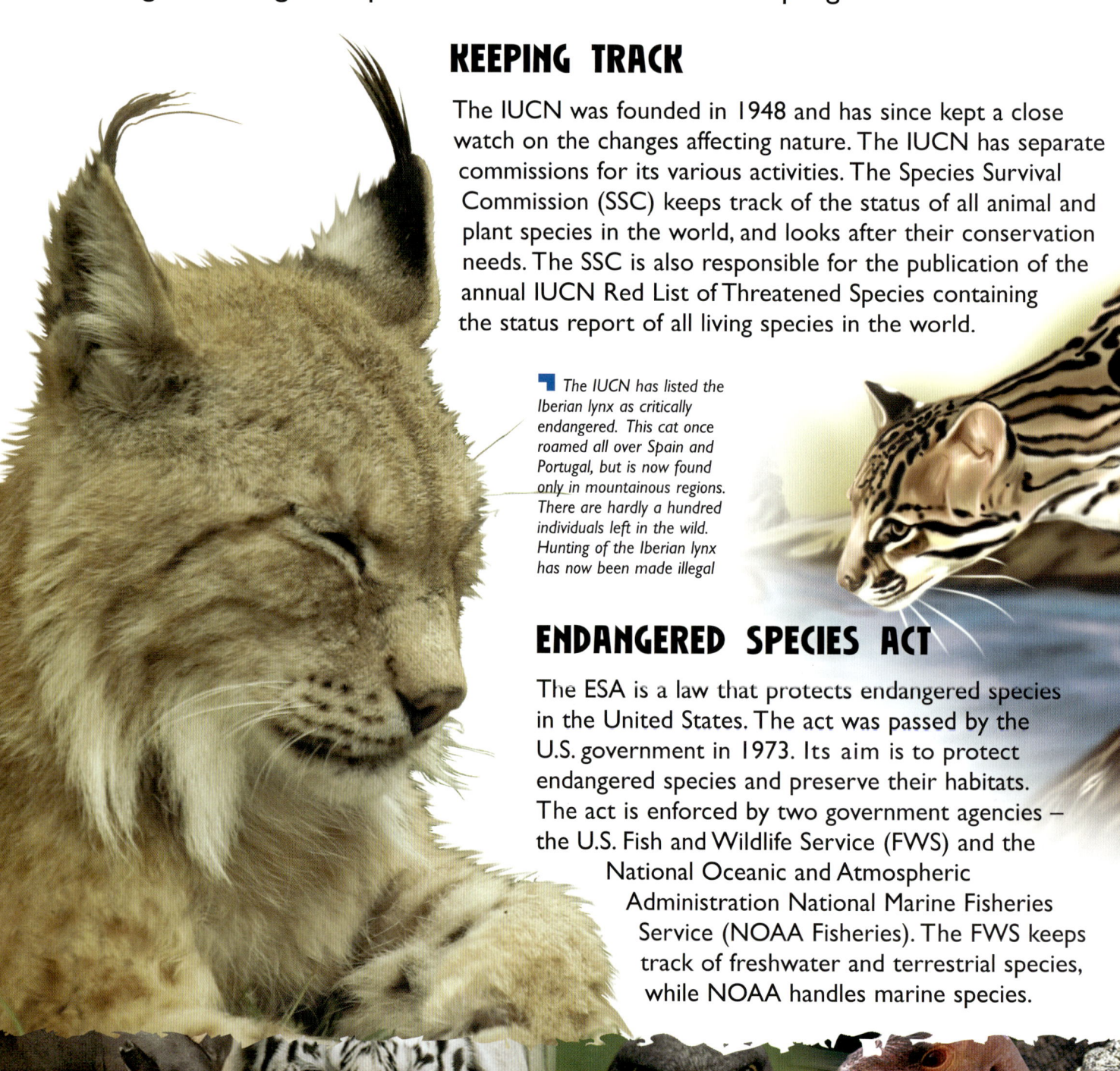

Keeping Track

The IUCN was founded in 1948 and has since kept a close watch on the changes affecting nature. The IUCN has separate commissions for its various activities. The Species Survival Commission (SSC) keeps track of the status of all animal and plant species in the world, and looks after their conservation needs. The SSC is also responsible for the publication of the annual IUCN Red List of Threatened Species containing the status report of all living species in the world.

◣ *The IUCN has listed the Iberian lynx as critically endangered. This cat once roamed all over Spain and Portugal, but is now found only in mountainous regions. There are hardly a hundred individuals left in the wild. Hunting of the Iberian lynx has now been made illegal*

Endangered Species Act

The ESA is a law that protects endangered species in the United States. The act was passed by the U.S. government in 1973. Its aim is to protect endangered species and preserve their habitats. The act is enforced by two government agencies – the U.S. Fish and Wildlife Service (FWS) and the National Oceanic and Atmospheric Administration National Marine Fisheries Service (NOAA Fisheries). The FWS keeps track of freshwater and terrestrial species, while NOAA handles marine species.

ENDANGERED ANIMALS

CONTROLLING TRADE

CITES is an agreement between the governments of the world aiming to control international trade in wild animals and plants. The organization keeps a close watch on illegal trades involving endangered species. It was brought into force in 1975. At the time, the significance of the agreement was not understood properly. Today, CITES has managed to save many species, including rhinos and tigers, from becoming extinct. It is illegal to trade in any animal, bird, or plant that has been listed under CITES. The species are listed in three appendices, according to the level of protection they require.

FACT FILE
IUCN Red List categories

Extinct
the last individual has died

Extinct in the wild
not occurring naturally – surviving only in captivity or breeding programs

Critically endangered
extremely high risk of extinction in the wild

Endangered
very high risk of extinction in the wild

Vulnerable
high risk of extinction in the wild

Near threatened
likely to qualify for a threatened category in the near future

Least concern
species available in abundance

Data deficient
inadequate information about distribution or population of a species

▟ The ocelot fur resembles that of a jaguar. This made the ocelot popular among hunters who hunted the small cat for its fur. The animal is now protected under the Endangered Species Act

▟ The California condor was once hunted extensively for its feathers and skin. Today, trading in condor skin has been made illegal by CITES

APES IN DANGER

The ape family is a diverse group that includes animals such as gorillas, chimpanzees, orangutans and gibbons. These highly intelligent animals are found in Asia and Africa. In the recent past, the numbers of apes in these regions have been reduced drastically. Today, almost all species of apes are regarded as the most endangered animals in the world.

POACHING

Hunters kill thousands of apes every year for meat. Some people consider ape meat a delicacy, while others eat ape meat when they have no other source of food. In places like Kalimantan in Borneo, Indonesia, people who lost their rice crops due to prolonged drought began hunting orangutans for their meat. In Africa, gorillas have been hunted for hundreds of years for both food and body parts. With the increase in human population, the number of gorillas hunted has also gone up in the last few years. In China and other Eastern countries, ape body parts are used in traditional medicines as well.

◀ In Africa, ape meat, or bushmeat, is very popular. Even today, African bushmen hunt apes for their meat

DESTRUCTION OF FORESTS

Habitat destruction is another major factor contributing to the decreasing ape population in Asia and Africa. People destroy rainforests for farming and building houses. The growing human population has led to the clearing of larger areas of forests. Large-scale logging has also reduced the forest cover. Without the dense protection of forests, apes not only lose their natural habitat, but are also more exposed to hunting.

◀ Forest fires are caused by long periods of heat and drought. People also set fires to clear the land for agriculture. The fire often spreads, destroying ape habitats

ENDANGERED ANIMALS

ILLEGAL PET TRADE

Infant apes are popular pets. Thousands of baby apes are caught every year for the pet trade. Adult apes are very protective about their children and never leave them unguarded. So poachers often kill the mother to capture the baby. Baby apes are sold to private collectors and zoos. The captured infant does not always survive. Poachers sometimes accidentally kill the baby along with its mother. Watching the mother killed can often result in the baby being frightened and traumatized for a long time. Moreover, baby apes are not strong and are easily infected by human illnesses.

▪ *Like human babies, baby apes need a lot of care. People often keep them in a poor environment. In such cases the baby ape falls ill and dies*

EXTINCT APE

A gigantic ape named *Gigantopithecus blackii*, or Black's giant ape, roamed the forests of Southeast Asia about 100,000 years ago. These large apes were about 10 feet tall and weighed a massive 1,200 pounds! It is believed that the *Gigantopithecus blackii* became extinct because of drastic climatic changes and competition for food.

FACT FILE
DECLINING IN THE WILD

WESTERN LOWLAND GORILLA – 94,000
MOUNTAIN GORILLA – 700
EASTERN LOWLAND GORILLA – 3,000
HAINAN BLACK-CRESTED GIBBON – 20
EASTERN BLACK-CRESTED GIBBON – 50
ORANGUTAN – 10,000-25,000
CHIMPANZEE – 150,000

RESCUING APES

The alarming decrease in ape populations over the last few years has led people to work hard towards protecting them. Laws have been enforced to prevent hunting and illegal pet trades. In some countries, large areas of forests have been set aside as reserves, making logging within these bounds illegal. Despite these strict measures, poachers continue to kill apes. Authorities are unable to keep a strict vigil on these offenders since most of them operate in the cover of dense forests. If the present situation continues, there will possibly be no apes left in the wild within the next 50 years, or even less.

▪ *Once found across the Asian continent, the orangutan is now restricted to the islands of Sumatra and Borneo*

Monkey Mania

Apes are not the only primates that have been endangered by the activities of man. Several species of monkeys are also in danger of becoming extinct in the near future. In fact, some monkeys are so close to becoming extinct that if nothing is done to protect them, they could be wiped off the face of the Earth within a couple of decades.

In the Name of Strength

In many Asian countries, like Vietnam, monkey meat is thought to make a person stronger and healthier. Thousands of monkeys were killed every year for their meat. Today, there are hardly any monkeys left in these regions. Monkeys were also hunted extensively for their medicinal value. Monkey bones, organs and tissues are used in traditional Asian medicine. The fur of some species of monkeys is also highly priced, making them targets for greedy poachers.

◼ The golden monkey, also called the snub-nosed monkey, found in the mountains of China, are killed for their bright orange fur and bones that are considered to have medicinal properties

Loss of Homes

Habitat loss is the biggest threat facing the monkeys of the world. Large parts of rainforests all over the world have already been converted into farming land. People continue to clear forests to make space for more houses, roads, dams and industries. Monkeys live in trees and depend on the thick forest cover for protection. Cutting down trees not only destroys their homes, but also exposes the monkeys to more danger. Apart from other animals and birds, these primates are also killed by humans, and they increasingly have nowhere to hide.

◼ Madagascar, an island off the southeast coast of Africa, has lost most of its rainforest, endangering the lemurs that cannot be found anywhere else in the world

ENDANGERED ANIMALS

Monkeys are also kept as pets. In many Asian countries, such as India, they are captured and trained to perform tricks

TO SAVE A PRIMATE

Several species of monkeys are now on the world's endangered list. Killing these monkeys for profit is illegal. The police and other law enforcement authorities are keeping an eye on illegal activities involving endangered species. Moreover, rainforests are being preserved to maintain a healthy population of these species. Conservationists are also fighting to regulate the use of monkeys as laboratory animals. Captive breeding programs are underway in the case of those species whose population is very low.

EXTINCT MONKEY

The *Protopithecus brasiliensis* was a large spider monkey and lived from about 2 million years to 10,000 years ago. Remains of this extinct primate found in Bahia, Brazil, indicate that this species was at least twice the size of an adult spider monkey. The remains suggest a weight of about 55 pounds (25 kilograms).

FACT FILE
Top ten endangered monkeys

Mentawai macaque
Delacour langur
Yellow-breasted capuchin
Red colobus
Tonkin snub-nosed monkey
Drill
Diana monkey
Proboscis monkey
Black snub-nosed monkey
Squirrel monkey

CATS ENDANGERED

Wild cats are another of the most endangered groups of animals in the world. The loss of their habitat is one of the biggest threats to the already dwindling population of wild cats. Hunting for their fur and body parts, and illegal pet trade have also contributed heavily to the present situation of these wild creatures.

JUMPING THE HOOP

A popular circus act consists of lions and panthers jumping through burning hoops. Such tricks do not come naturally to these animals, they have to be taught to perform them. Wild cats are not easily trained like dogs. Trainers often beat and starve these animals to make them learn the tricks. Cats that are either too stubborn or too old to perform are killed, caged for good, or beaten and abandoned to die. The use of animals in circus acts is on the decline due to pressure by animal rights activists.

▏*White tigers are very rare in the wild. Most white tigers that are seen in zoos have been bred in captivity. Two white tigers are usually bred to ensure a white offspring. However, white tigers suffer from many health problems and struggle to survive in the wild*

LETHAL TRADE

Wild cats-even big ones like lions and tigers-are sometimes sold as pets. People buy the cute and cuddly cubs thinking they would make good pets. This illusion is often shattered as the cat outgrows its small cage and becomes expensive to feed and maintain. They are then abandoned near woodlands or in animal shelter homes. Most of these cats are unhealthy and badly injured, often dying before they can be rescued. Some owners cut the claws of the cats so that they cannot attack. When such cats are abandoned, they are not even able to defend themselves when attacked by other animals. If the claws are not cut properly, it can also cause infection and cripple the cat permanently.

JUST FOR FUR

Wild cats are widely killed for their fur. The furs of bobcats and lynxes are still used to make fashionable coats. Wild cats are also hunted for their body parts. In traditional Asian medicine, tiger parts are thought to cure diseases like rheumatism and dysentery. Bones of wild cats are used to make jewelery and other souvenirs, too. People also kill wild cats to defend themselves. Wild cats have a reputation as ferocious killers. This has led to the killing of many lions, leopards and tigers in Asia and Africa. The growing human population has also led to encroachment onto the territories of wild cats. Today, people live very close to these animals, which attack cattle when there is a shortage of prey.

◾ Wild cats were also hunted for sport

EXTINCT CAT

The sabre-toothed cat, or *Smilodon*, lived about 3 million to 10,000 years ago. This close relative of the modern big cats was found in North and South America. It had two knife-like fangs that were about 7 inches (17 cm) long. It had powerful legs and a short tail, and was nearly two times heavier than the lion.

FACT FILE
ENDANGERED CATS

SPANISH LYNX
SNOW LEOPARD
TIGER
FLORIDA COUGAR
CHEETAH
ASIATIC LION
LEOPARD
JAGUAR
BOBCAT

TO THE RESCUE

Wild cats are now protected in most countries, making it illegal to kill them. Pet trade and fur made from the skin of endangered cats have been banned in many places. Breeding of wild cats for fur, meat and pet trade has also been banned. In most countries, it is against the law to keep a wild cat as a pet. However, some countries allow people to keep pet wild cats with a proper license. Parts of forests where wild cats live have been turned into national parks and wildlife reserves, to protect these areas from being destroyed by humans.

◾ *The Masai warriors of Africa used to hunt lions to prove their courage and manhood. This ritual is now illegal as the lion is a protected species*

CROCODILIANS

The crocodilian family includes crocodiles and its relatives — alligators, gavials (gharials) and caimans. Crocodilians have been around for millions of years. They existed even during the Age of Dinosaurs. Among certain communities, crocodiles were considered holy. However, this has not stopped humans from driving these species to near extinction.

DRIVEN BY FEAR

In some places, crocodiles and their relatives are considered a pest. In many parts of the United States, the American alligator was hunted extensively to protect cattle. This problem is increasing as humans expand into more crocodile habitats. In Africa, crocodiles were killed during European colonisation. The new settlers felt threatened by these huge reptiles and killed them in large numbers.

▪ Shoes, bags and other leather products made from crocodile hide are still in demand, although crocodile hunting is now controlled

▪ The Nile crocodile was hunted into near extinction

VALUED FOR HIDE

The biggest threat to crocodilians today is the high demand for their hide, or leather. Caiman hide was particularly popular because of its beautiful patterns. At one point, about one million caimans were killed every year to meet the high demands for their leather. Hunters used rifles, spotlights and powerboats to acquire crocodile hide of the highest quality. Apart from their hide, crocodilians are also killed for oil and meat. In some places like Madagascar, crocodile oil is believed to cure burns, skin problems and even cancer.

ENDANGERED ANIMALS

TO SAVE A CROC

Today, all 23 species of crocodilians are in danger of becoming extinct. Seven of these species are already critically endangered and could be wiped out any day. Many steps have been taken to save these creatures. The killing of crocodiles for the making of leather goods is now controlled. Alligator and crocodile farms have been set up to breed crocodilians for this purpose. Crocodile habitats are also being preserved in many countries to protect these animals.

EXTINCT CROCODILE

The extinct *Deinosuchus* was the largest crocodile in the world. This 'terrible crocodile' lived alongside the dinosaurs, about 70 million years ago. A skull of the *Deinosuchus*, found in Texas, is over 6 feet (2 m) long. Scientists believe that this gigantic croc grew to about 50 feet (15 m) in length! Modern crocodiles grow to a maximum of 20 feet.

FACT FILE
ENDANGERED CROCODILIANS

Philippine crocodile
Siamese crocodile
Chinese alligator
Cuban crocodile
Tomistoma
Orinoco crocodile
Gharial

▎ The huge demand for the hide of crocodiles and alligators is now being met by breeding farms set up specially for that purpose

Other Reptilians

Like crocodiles, turtles, lizards and snakes are also being threatened with extinction. Many species of lizards are on the endangered list, while all seven species of marine turtles are in danger of being wiped from the face of the Earth.

▸ *People usually kill snakes out of fear. Some, like the Indian python, are also killed for their skin*

Turtle Tragedy

Turtles are most vulnerable to extinction. This is because their eggs and meat are popular delicacies. Turtle eggs fall victim to both humans and animals. Humans also hunt these creatures for their shells, which are used to make jewellery, hair combs and other souvenirs. Products made from turtle skin are very popular. Turtle shell is also used in traditional Asian medicines. Oil from certain species of turtles is used in medicines and caulking boats. Large numbers of marine turtles are caught in fishing nets and drown. They also die by swallowing floating plastic, which they mistake for their favourite food – jellyfish.

▸ *Green sea turtles have been hunted in large numbers for their fat – called* calipee *– which is used to make turtle soup*

Lizards and Snakes

One of the biggest threats facing lizards and snakes is the growing market for exotic pets. If the current trend continues, certain species of lizards and snakes would be seen only in private homes. Snakes like pythons and some large lizard species are also killed for their skin, which is used to make shoes and bags. Snakeskin boots were at one time very fashionable. Today, it is illegal to kill certain species of snakes for their skin. Snakes are also killed for their meat and blood. In Asian countries like Thailand, snake blood is considered to have medicinal properties.

▸ *The Komodo dragon is found only in a few Indonesian islands. Its limited range has made this reptile vulnerable to extinction*

ENDANGERED ANIMALS

IN SEARCH OF HOME

All reptiles suffer greatly from habitat loss. Human activity in regions once dominated by these creatures is increasing. Destruction of forests has led to their exposure to the outside world. These creatures have nowhere to hide and often fall prey to birds and other predators. Additionally, humans kill snakes out of fear. Coastal development has led to destruction of the nesting grounds of turtles. New born turtles, attracted by bright lights on the beaches, tend to move towards the source and are often killed in the process.

▶ People who frequent beaches often unknowingly stamp on turtle eggs

FACT FILE
ENDANGERED REPTILES

Loggerhead sea turtle
Green sea turtle
Mesoamerican river turtle
Leatherback sea turtle
Hawksbill sea turtle
Burmese start tortoise
Olive ridley turtle
Grand skink
Komodo dragon
Indian python
Lake Erie water snake
Western diamondback rattlesnake
King cobra
Blue racer snake

EXTINCT TURTLE

The giant marine turtle *Archelon ischyros* lived about 70 million years ago. It is believed to be a relative of the modern leatherback sea turtle. It had paddle-like legs and a shell with a leathery covering or a horny plate over it. The *Archelon* was about 13-16 feet (4-5 m) long and just its shell could measure 7 feet (2 m)! They probably became extinct due to climatic changes.

Endangering the Elephant

The elephant is the largest living land animal. In many Asian countries, the elephant plays an important role in religion. Its size and strength have also made it one of the most important symbols of royalty, yet this gentle giant is, unfortunately, among the most endangered species in the world today.

Alarming Decline

There are two main types of elephants in the world – the African elephant and the Asian elephant. The African elephant is considered a threatened species, while the Asian species is classified as endangered. African elephants were once found throughout Africa, while the Asian variety roamed the forests ranging from Syria to northern China and Indonesia. Today, African elephants are found mainly south of the Sahara Desert, while Asian elephants have been reduced to a few numbers in India, Sri Lanka, the Malay Peninsula, Borneo and parts of Southeast Asia. The reasons for this alarming decline in elephant populations are numerous. As is the case with other animals, humans are the biggest villains here.

▌ In countries like India, elephants are tamed for use in circuses and temples

All for Ivory!

Hunting has always been the biggest threat to elephants. People used to hunt elephants for sport. This became worse following the growing demand for ivory, of which the elephant tusk is made. Ivory is smooth, beautiful and lasts a long time. This made it a popular material for jewellery and other artefacts, including furniture. Even when hunting was banned, people poached elephants due to the high price that a pair of tusks fetched. Apart from causing their numbers to decline, poaching has also affected the social structure of elephants.

▌ Ivory is also known as 'white gold' due to its high price

ENDANGERED ANIMALS

FIGHTING FOR SPACE

Elephants are huge and need a lot of space and food. For many years, people have been cutting down trees to make space for farming and housing. This has led to a considerable reduction in space for elephants. Moreover, wild elephants do not make good neighbours. They tend to destroy crops and are even known to attack humans. Male elephants in particular are very violent during the mating season. Villagers often kill such elephants out of fear.

Poachers usually target adult elephants. This has left many elephant herds without parents. The young elephants are left helpless, with no adults to show them the migration routes and teach them where to find water during the dry season

EXTINCT ELEPHANT

Mammoths lived from about 1.6 million years ago to 10,000 years ago. They had long, curved tusks. The largest are believed to have attained a shoulder height of 14 feet (4m).
The *woolly mammoth* evolved later and, with its body covered in long hair, was better suited to adapt to the Ice Age. Most *mammoths* died by the end of the Ice Age.

FACT FILE
Declining numbers

West African elephant – under 10,000
African forest elephant – about 60,000
African savannah elephant – about 400,000
Asian elephant – about 50,000
in the wild

Feathered Friends

There are about 10,000 known species of birds in the world. More than 1,200 species are endangered, threatened, or vulnerable. Like all animals, birds too have been affected by habitat loss, hunting, predation and pollution.

No Place to Nest

Cutting down trees affects birds the most. Most birds build their nests in trees. This is mainly done to protect the eggs and chicks from predators. When trees are cut to make way for farming and houses, the birds lose their homes. In such cases, birds build nests on rooftops and high buildings. This increases the risk of the eggs and chicks falling to their death or being robbed by people. Birds are also hunted for various reasons. Some are hunted for their meat, while others are hunted for sport. Some, like eagles and vultures, are killed to protect domestic animals and birds.

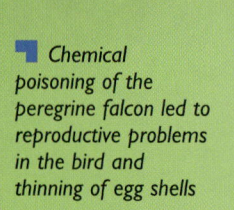

▪ Chemical poisoning of the peregrine falcon led to reproductive problems in the bird and thinning of egg shells

▪ Many birds like the Golden Eagle were once considered to be pests and therefore killed in large numbers

Poisoned Food

While consuming food, birds can sometimes take in poisonous chemicals used in factories and as fertilizers for crops. The effects of chemical poisoning are most pronounced among raptors, which are at the top of the food chain. Raptors feed on small animals and birds. The latter, in turn, feed on smaller animals or plants. Any poison found in the animals and plants at the bottom of the food chain gets collected. By the time the poison reaches the raptor's prey, the amount of poison can be quite high.

ENDANGERED ANIMALS

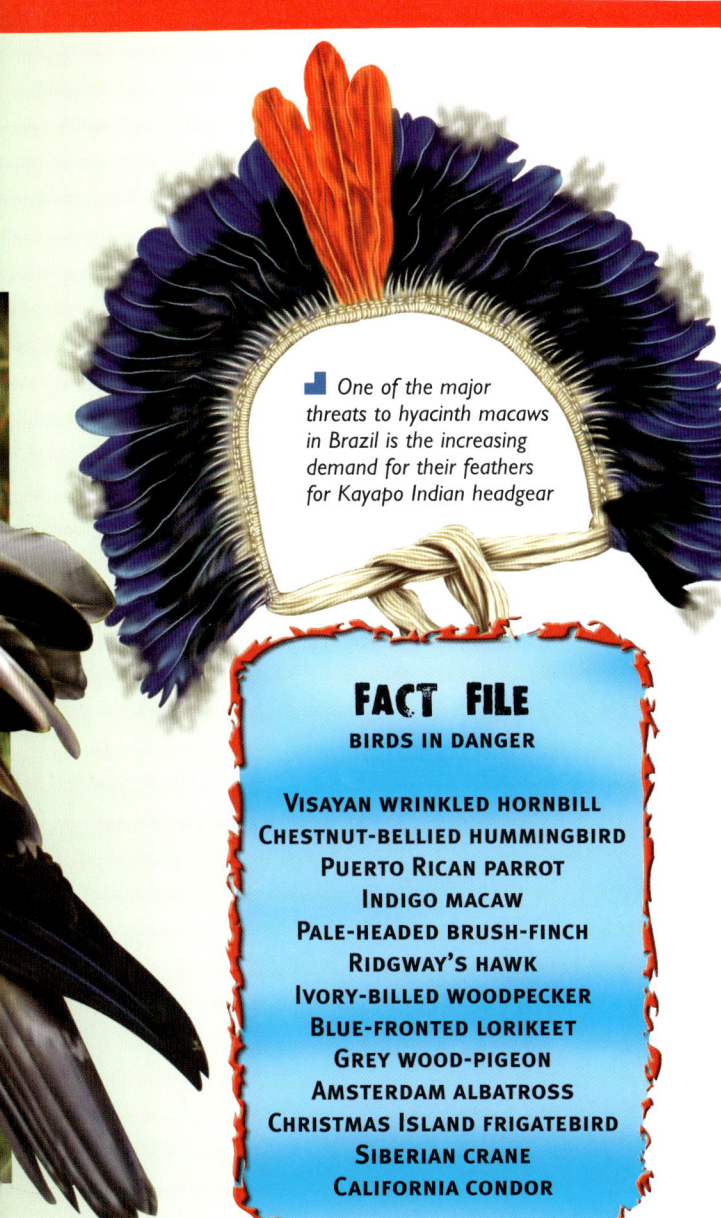

PET TRADE

You must have seen parrots, macaws and other tropical birds kept as pets. However, did you know that these birds are in so much demand that soon they could be extinct in the wild? Some of the rarer tropical birds fetch a large amount of money. This encourages poachers to capture these birds even if it is against the law. Poachers often cut down trees to take the chicks from the nest. This is particularly harmful since some species do not even breed every year. Moreover, a majority of the chicks die before they even reach the pet store!

◼ One of the major threats to hyacinth macaws in Brazil is the increasing demand for their feathers for Kayapo Indian headgear

FACT FILE
BIRDS IN DANGER

Visayan wrinkled hornbill
Chestnut-bellied hummingbird
Puerto Rican parrot
Indigo macaw
Pale-headed brush-finch
Ridgway's hawk
Ivory-billed woodpecker
Blue-fronted lorikeet
Grey wood-pigeon
Amsterdam albatross
Christmas Island frigatebird
Siberian crane
California condor

EXTINCT BIRD

The passenger pigeon was once the most abundant bird on the planet. In the beginning of the 19th century there were about five billion passenger pigeons in North America. By the 20th century, humans had hunted them to extinction. The forests where these birds nested were destroyed. The birds themselves were hunted for their meat, which was used to make pigeon pie.

CONSERVATION EFFORTS

Over 1,200 bird species have been listed as endangered. Strict laws have been adopted to save these birds from extinction. Hunting or capturing any of the endangered species is illegal. Owning any as pets is punishable. Killing these birds for their feathers and trading in any such feathered articles has been banned. Rare birds are also being bred and re-introduced into forests after training them for life in the wilderness.

◼ The American bald eagle was one of the raptors in the United States that was affected by the excessive use of pesticides like DDT. Today, the ban imposed on use of DDT has helped to bring this species back from the brink of extinction.

Flightless Birds in Danger

Flightless birds have wings, but they have lost the ability to fly. It is thought that since most of these birds lived in places with hardly any mammals, they had few enemies and so did not feel the need to fly. Over many years, these birds probably forgot how to fly! Today, their inability to fly has put some of them on the brink of extinction.

New Predators

Most flightless birds are found on islands or in places where there were few or no land animals. In subsequent years, though, humans inhabited many of these places and brought with them land animals such as monkeys, dogs and cats. Suddenly, the flightless birds had to defend themselves from both human and animal predators. Since they could not fly, these creatures found it difficult to escape being hunted. This is one of the main reasons for the drastic fall in the populations of certain flightless birds.

◼ *Kakapo, the world's only flightless parrot is a native of New Zealand. There are only about 86 Kakapos in the world today*

◼ *Oil spills and fishing nets pose a major threat to flightless birds like penguins*

Easy Prey

Flightless birds can be captured easily. This made them easy prey for hunters. People killed these birds for their meat and feathers. The penguin was hunted for its oil and skin. Until recently, people collected guano (bird excretion) of penguins as it was considered a good fertilizer. In the process, people damaged the bird's nests and eggs. Guano collection was so popular during the last two centuries that it had a most adverse effect on the penguin population. Pollution and sudden climatic changes have also contributed to the rapid decline of flightless birds by killing or driving away their prey. Many birds have died because of lack of food.

ENDANGERED ANIMALS

▪ Many species of kiwis are listed as endangered. These flightless birds are specially affected by animals like weasels and cats that were introduced into their habitats by humans

FACT FILE
Flightless birds at risk

Kakapo
Campbell Island teal
Brown kiwi
Takahe
Auckland Island rail
New Zealand bush wren
Humboldt penguin
Galapagos penguin
Yellow-eyed penguin
Erect-crested penguin

FIGHTING FOR SURVIVAL

The threat faced by flightless birds has prompted conservationists to take an active interest in preserving these species. Many species have been taken from their dangerous surroundings and resettled on islands free of predators and safe for their survival. Many others are being bred in captivity and then gradually re-introduced into the wild. This not only ensures the safety of the eggs, but also the protection of chicks from predators. Guano mining and egg collection have been restricted. Trade in live birds has also been made illegal.

EXTINCT FLIGHTLESS BIRD

Aepyornis, or the elephant bird, was a large flightless bird that inhabited the island of Madagascar. These birds existed until about 500 years ago. *Aepyornis* was the world's largest bird. It was believed to be over 10 feet (3 m) tall and more than 1,100 pounds (500 kg) in weight. It is thought to have given rise to the legends of the roc, a huge bird that could even carry elephants.

Bears on the Brink

There are eight species of bears in the world. They are the Malayan sun bear, polar bear, grizzly bear, Asiatic black bear, American black bear, giant panda, sloth bear and spectacled bear. Most of these are struggling to survive in the modern world. The challenges they face are not small. The kind of dangers these animals face is so huge that it is a wonder that bears are not already extinct.

Bears in Jeopardy

As with all other animals, humans are the biggest enemy of bears. They hunt bears for fun as well as for their fur and body parts. Bear fat, gallbladder, meat, paws, spinal cord, bones and blood are a vital part of traditional Asian medicines. They are thought to cure various diseases. In Taiwan, sun bear paws are used to make soup. The pelt of giant pandas is used to make expensive sleeping mats. People who live near woodlands consider bears to be a nuisance and often kill them to protect their crops and livestock.

■ Sloth bears make good entertainers and are caught in great numbers for this purpose

■ Loss of habitat is the main cause for the declining populations of the giant panda

No Food, No Home

Bears are most affected by habitat destruction and pollution. The logging industry is largely responsible for the destruction of forests that are home to most bears. Pollution and drastic climatic changes also affect bear populations, especially in the Arctic region – the home of the polar bears. These bears hunt on the ice floes of the Arctic. When ice melts early due to changes in climatic conditions, it becomes difficult for polar bears to find food. They are also hunted by the locals for their meat and luxurious fur.

ENDANGERED ANIMALS

SAVE THE BEARS

Today, many bear species are protected and trade in bear products has been banned. Parts of forests have been preserved to protect bear habitats. Captive breeding is another popular method of conservation. In China, bear farms have developed a new method of extracting bile from gallbladders of live bears, thus reducing the number of bears killed just for their galls. Killing bears for sport or for their body parts is now illegal.

▗ *Oil spills and chemical pollution affect the growth and survival of polar bear cubs*

FACT FILE
ENDANGERED BEARS

GIANT PANDA
MALAYAN SUN BEAR
ASIATIC BLACK BEAR
SLOTH BEAR
SPECTACLED BEAR
POLAR BEAR

EXTINCT BEAR

One of the best known extinct bears is the *great cave bear*. This bear became extinct about 10,000 years ago, probably due to climatic changes or even widespread hunting by humans. The remains of this species have been found in caves throughout Europe. The *great cave bear* was as large as the modern brown bear and lived on a largely vegetarian diet.

Endangered Antelopes

There are about 90 species of antelopes in the world. Of these, about 15 species are endangered and the rest are threatened or vulnerable. Most antelope species are found in Africa. Years of war, mining, logging and poaching have contributed to the rapid decline in antelope populations across the continent.

LIFE IN THE DARK CONTINENT

Antelope species in Africa have suffered greatly due to illegal poaching. Most species are hunted for their meat and precious horns, which are used in traditional Asian medicine. Habitat loss is also a major threat as antelopes find it difficult to compete with domestic animals like cattle for grazing land. Overgrazing has led to less food for the antelopes, forcing them to migrate far from home in search of greener pastures. This forced migration has caused the death of many antelopes. They have also been killed in the crossfire of various wars in Africa.

■ *The scimitar-horned oryx was once found in large numbers in the desert of Sahara. Overhunting has made this species critically endangered*

HUNTED FOR FUN

Antelopes have also been hunted for fun. Their speed and agility have made them popular victims of game hunting. Certain species of antelopes are frequently sent to Texas, where game hunting is a popular sport. There are ranches in Texas that breed antelopes solely for this sport, commonly known as canned hunting. In these hunts, hunters pay to kill a captive antelope within a fenced property. The hunter is allowed to take back his trophy, usually the head, as proof of his achievement. Astonishingly, some of the species of antelopes currently offered to trophy hunters are on the endangered list!

ENDANGERED ANIMALS

WOOLLY TALES

Some species have been targeted for their soft, warm wool. The Tibetan antelope, or chiru, is one such species that has been hunted almost to extinction for its wool. The undercoat of the chiru is extremely soft and, therefore, sought after. It is called '*shahtoosh*', meaning 'the pleasure of kings' in Persian and can be obtained only by killing the animal. So, hunters lay leg-hold traps and when an antelope gets trapped, the hunter shoots it dead. The undercoat is then cut off to make exquisite woollen garments. The chiru is protected by Chinese law, but because there is such a high demand for shahtoosh in the west, large scale poaching is responsible for the slaughter of thousands of the animals every year.

EXTINCT ANTELOPE

The *bluebuck*, or blue antelope, was the first large African mammal to become extinct in recent times. Once found in large numbers in South Africa, the *bluebuck* population had already decreased when the Europeans first arrived here. The new settlers hunted the animal extensively, using its habitat for agriculture. The *bluebuck* became an extinct species around 1800.

▶ *Shahtoosh shawls, made from the wool of the Tibetan antelope, also known as chiru, are so soft that they can be passed through a wedding ring. Therefore, these shawls are also known as "ring shawls". Five to seven chirus have to be killed to make just one shawl. Until recently, about 20,000 of these animals were killed every year for their pelts*

FACT FILE
ANTELOPE IN DANGER

Addax
Saiga antelope
Arabian Oryx
Scimitar-horned oryx
Tibetan antelope
Mountain nyala
Cuvier's gazelle
Rhim gazelle
Dama gazelle
Przewalski's gazelle

▶ *Canned hunts are a profitable business in Texas even today. Sometimes certain zoos that run out of space sell adult animals to canned hunting facilities*

RHINOS ON THE RUN

The rhinoceros and its relatives, the tapir and the zebra, are gravely in danger of extinction. These animals are victims of both deforestation and human greed. The rhinoceros has been overhunted for its horn, while tapirs and zebras are hunted for their meat and skin.

▰ Half of the world's rhinoceroses disappeared during the 1970s. Today, less than 20,000 rhinos exist in the world

RHINOS

All five species of rhinos are on the brink of extinction because they have been hunted extensively for their precious horn. Although the Indian rhino and the white rhino seem to be recovering, the Javan, Sumatran and black rhinos are considered to be critically endangered. A major decline in rhino population occurred in the 1970s, due to an increase in global oil prices. In the Arab country of Yemen, rhino horns, considered to be a status symbol, were used to make decorative handles of daggers. The rise in oil price made the people of Yemen, which had lots of oil, very rich. Soon, people were able to afford rhino horns causing a sudden increase in the demand for this product.

TAPIRS AND ZEBRAS

There are four species of tapirs in the world and all of them are near extinction. These animals are found in the rainforests of Malaysia and Central America. Mountain tapirs are listed as endangered mainly due to the clearing of forests for farming activities. They were also hunted for their meat. Like tapirs, zebras also have been affected by deforestation. Of the three existing species, the mountain zebra and Grevy's zebra are endangered. Apart from habitat loss, both were killed for their skin. The skin of Grevy's zebra with its narrow stripes was especially popular for making handbags, rugs, slippers and even clothes.

▰ Some native tribes use the hooves and snout of the tapir as a cure for heart problems and epilepsy.

ENDANGERED ANIMALS

CONSERVATION ATTEMPTS

Conservationists have been working hard to save the rhinoceros and its relatives from extinction. In some cases, their hard work has paid off. However, not all species are completely safe from human greed. Although it is illegal to kill rhinoceroses, tapirs and zebras for commercial gain, people continue to poach these animals and sell their products on the black market.
In Africa, the black rhinoceros populations have declined so much that, today, armed guards accompany these animals while they graze in sanctuaries. The horn of this rhinoceros is so profitable that sometimes hunters even resort to attacking the guards to get the horn.

▎ *The horns of rhinoceroses were believed to act against certain poisons and have been used in traditional Asian medicines for thousands of years*

EXTINCT RHINO

The *woolly rhino* was a close relative of the modern Sumatran rhino. It was once found in northern Europe and eastern Asia. This rhino had two horns and its body was covered with thick hair. It grazed on grass and shrubs. It lived during the Ice Age and was probably hunted by early humans. The species became extinct about 10,000 years ago.

FACT FILE
On the road to extinction

Java rhinoceros
only about 70 left

Sumatran rhinoceros
only about 300 left

Indian rhino
only about 2,400 left

Black rhinoceros
only about 3,610 left

White rhinoceros
over 11,330 left

Grevy's zebra
fewer than 6,000 left

Mountain zebra
only about 14,000 left

Mountain tapir
fewer than 2,500 left

CANINES IN DANGER

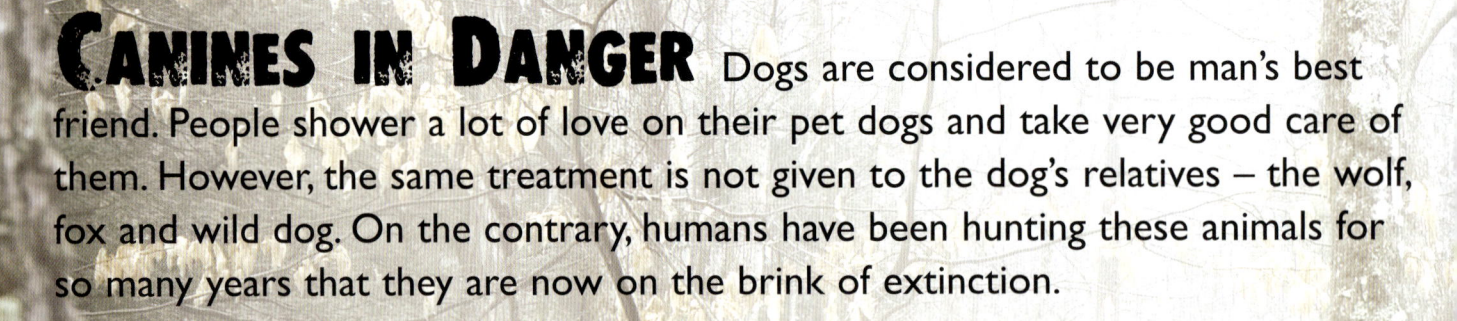

Dogs are considered to be man's best friend. People shower a lot of love on their pet dogs and take very good care of them. However, the same treatment is not given to the dog's relatives – the wolf, fox and wild dog. On the contrary, humans have been hunting these animals for so many years that they are now on the brink of extinction.

FIGHTING FOR SPACE

The biggest threat facing wolves, wild dogs and foxes is habitat loss. Vast areas of forests and woodlands have been destroyed to make way for farm lands and houses, leading to a direct competition for survival between these animals and humans. Thousands of wolves and foxes have been shot to protect domestic animals and birds, or simply out of fear. Moreover, several myths and superstitions are attached to wolves making them unwelcome near human populations.

LACK OF PREY

Wolves, foxes and wild dogs have also been affected by the decline in the number of prey. Human encroachment on forestland and overhunting have greatly reduced the prey population. Wolves, wild dogs and foxes often have to fight with other wild animals like hyenas, leopards and tigers for prey. The bigger animals usually win leaving the wild canines to die of starvation. Desperate and hungry, these animals sometimes attack humans or resort to hunting down farm animals for food.

▙ Habitat loss and the decline in prey populations pose the greatest threat to the survival of the dhole, a species of wild dog from southern Asia.

DISEASES

The wild canines are very vulnerable to diseases. The increasing human presence in their habitats has brought wild canines into contact with domestic dogs. This, in turn, has increased the risk of infections. Wild canines are easily infected by diseases like canine distemper and rabies. These diseases spread fast among the rest of the population, sometimes killing all members of a pack.

EXTINCT WOLF

The Falkland Islands wolf was once found on the islands by the same name. It was up to 35 inches long and had a soft, dense coat that was brownish-grey in color. When Spanish settlers came to the island, they poisoned the wolves to protect their cattle. The wolf was also hunted extensively in the 1830s for its dense fur. The last wolf is believed to have been killed in 1876.

► Large numbers of Ethiopian wolves have died due to rabies contracted from domestic dogs in the past. This has now been controlled by vaccinating the wolves against the disease. However, cross breeding with domestic dogs continues to be a problem and might eventually wipe out the species

FACT FILE
ENDANGERED SPECIES

RED WOLF
ETHIOPIAN WOLF
ASIATIC WILD DOG
AFRICAN WILD DOG
CALIFORNIA CHANNEL ISLAND FOX
DARWIN'S FOX

STORY OF SURVIVAL

The story of the gray wolf is one of the most encouraging tales of survival in the history of conservation. The gray wolf once roamed all over North America. However, in the 19th century the wolf gained the reputation of being a killing machine. Soon, bounty hunters were being employed to hunt the 'monster' down. By the end of the 19th century, about two million gray wolves had been mercilessly slaughtered. In 1974, the animal was listed as endangered under the Endangered Species Acts of the United States. A couple of decades later, gray wolf populations began to increase – giving hope to thousands of other endangered species.

► By the mid-1900s the gray wolf population had either reduced or disappeared from most of its ranges including protected areas like the Yellowstone National Park

WHALES ON THE EDGE

There are over 70 species of whales and dolphins in the world. This also includes the 13 species belonging to the great whale family, of which seven have been listed as endangered or vulnerable. Many river dolphins are also considered endangered.

WHALING INTO EXTINCTION

The great whales include huge whales like blue whales, right whales, humpback whales, fin whales and gray whales. In the 19th and early 20th centuries, these whales were hunted for their meat and the oil from their blubber. Before electric lights came into operation, whale oil was used to light lamps. This led to widespread whaling. The great whales were targeted because of the large amount of oil and meat that could be obtained from them. Earlier, whale oil was also used to make many items including candles and lipsticks!

▪ *The right whale is the most affected by whaling. This whale is a very slow swimmer and prefers to stay near the water surface, making it very vulnerable. Whalers gave this species its name, as they considered it the "right" whale to hunt*

OTHER THREATS

Today, despite various measures taken to curb whaling, it is still being done illegally. Modern threats to whale population include pollution, fishing gear and ship strikes. Oil slicks and chemicals from ships and industries running into the ocean not only harm whales, but also kill their food source. Toxic chemicals get collected in the blubber of adult whales and are passed on to their young through milk. The calves are too weak to withstand the poison and usually die. Many whales die by colliding with ships.

▪ *Another major threat to whale population is entanglement in fishing nets or lines. Whales often accidentally get caught in fishing nets and drown*

ENDANGERED ANIMALS

SAVING THE WHALES

In 1946, 14 countries joined together to form the International Whaling Commission (IWC) to check widespread whaling. In 1986 the commission declared a worldwide ban on whaling for commercial purposes. A ban has also been imposed on whale products. Today, only certain whales, like minke whales, are allowed to be caught. Even then, a limit has been set for the number of whales that can be killed. This has been done to enable whales to replenish their population.

EXTINCT WHALE

The *Pakicetus inachus* was a whale that resembled a seal. It lived about 50 million years ago. It was about 6 feet (1.8 m) long and was believed to have lived both on land and in water. The *Pakicetus inachus* had small rear flippers and a pointed tail with no flukes. Fossils of this whale have been found in Pakistan.

FACT FILE
ENDANGERED WHALES

- RIGHT WHALE
- BOWHEAD WHALE
- BLUE WHALE
- FIN WHALE
- HUMPBACK WHALE
- SEI WHALE
- SPERM WHALE
- VAQUITA
- BAIJI
- INDUS RIVER DOLPHIN

▶ *By the 1920s, commercial whaling had made the California gray whale almost extinct. However, gray populations have been on the rise ever since this species was brought under the protection of the IWC. Today, special care is taken to protect the gray whale breeding grounds at Baja, California. This includes restricted entry of boats in and around the breeding lagoons*

▶ *Although whaling has been banned, right whale population is not recovering as these great whales continue to be victims of collisions with boats and fishing net entanglements. The Northern Right Whale is the most affected with hardly 300 individuals in existence*

Sharks Endangered

More than a hundred million sharks are killed each year, leading to an alarming decline in their numbers. Unlike other fish, sharks do not have babies until they are old. Even then, some female sharks give birth to only 2-3 pups at a time. This is not enough to replace the sharks that are killed every year, making them vulnerable to extinction. If sharks continue to be killed at the current rate, there will soon be none left in the oceans!

Shark Trade

Sharks are endangered due for many reasons, but the one that has affected the shark population the most is over-fishing. Sharks are often killed for their meat, hide and teeth. Shark hide is used to make bags and shoes, while their teeth are used to make jewelery. Shark cartilage powder is believed by some to prevent cancer and shark liver oil is also thought to have medicinal properties. Some sharks, like the great white, are hunted for sport! The jaws and teeth of the great white are collected like trophies. However, cage diving is now slowly replacing game fishing. People go into the water in cages to see live sharks up close. They use a mixture of blood and fish parts, called 'chum', to attract the sharks.

▪ Cage diving is considered to change the natural behavior of the shark. It is believed to increase the number of shark attacks since more sharks are attracted towards the coast and they become more familiar with humans. Moreover, the "chum" may cause fatal infections

Finning for Profit

In Asian countries such as China, dried shark fins are used to make a very expensive soup. Fishermen capture sharks, cut their fins off and throw them back into the sea to bleed to death. These fins fetch a lot of money – making 'finning' a profitable business. Shark species that are most hunted for their fins are hammerheads, mako, blue sharks, basking and whale sharks.

▪ Although finning is banned in most countries today, the demand for shark fin soup is still high, encouraging fishermen to engage in illegal finning

ENDANGERED ANIMALS

PAINFUL DEATH

Sometimes sharks are caught accidentally when fishermen drag nets through the water to catch other fish. Sharks caught in this manner are often let go, but most of them die before this can be done. Fishing boats sometimes abandon nets in the sea. Sharks get entangled in these nets and die.

▪ Some fishermen use hooked lines to catch fish. When a shark is hooked instead of a fish, the line is cut off to let the shark go. But the hook usually remains in the shark's jaw causing it a lot of pain and preventing feeding. If swallowed, the hook will cause internal injuries leading to a slow and painful death

EXTINCT SHARK

Sharks have been around for more than 400 million years! Many ancient species are now extinct. The best known among these is the *Megalodon*, a giant shark that grew to a length of 40 feet (12 m). Its teeth were three times as large as those of the great white. Scientists believe that the *Megalodon* became extinct due to drastic changes in weather and lack of food.

FACT FILE
ENDANGERED SHARKS

GANGES SHARK
BORNEO SHARK
BASKING SHARK
BLACKTIP SHARK
GREY NURSE SHARK
GREAT WHITE SHARK
WHALE SHARK
PORBEAGLE SHARK
OTHBACK ANGEL SHARK
HITEFIN TOPESHARK

SAVE THE SHARK

The hunting of many endangered species such as whale sharks, basking sharks and great white sharks has been banned in most countries. Fishermen have to obtain a fishing permit to catch even those sharks that are not in the endangered list. Authorities regulate the number of sharks that can be killed. Sharks are also tagged and released for scientific studies. Tagging not only helps to keep track of the individual shark and learn more about its habits, but also makes sure that the shark is protected.

▪ *Megalodon's tooth*

SEALS AND SEA COWS

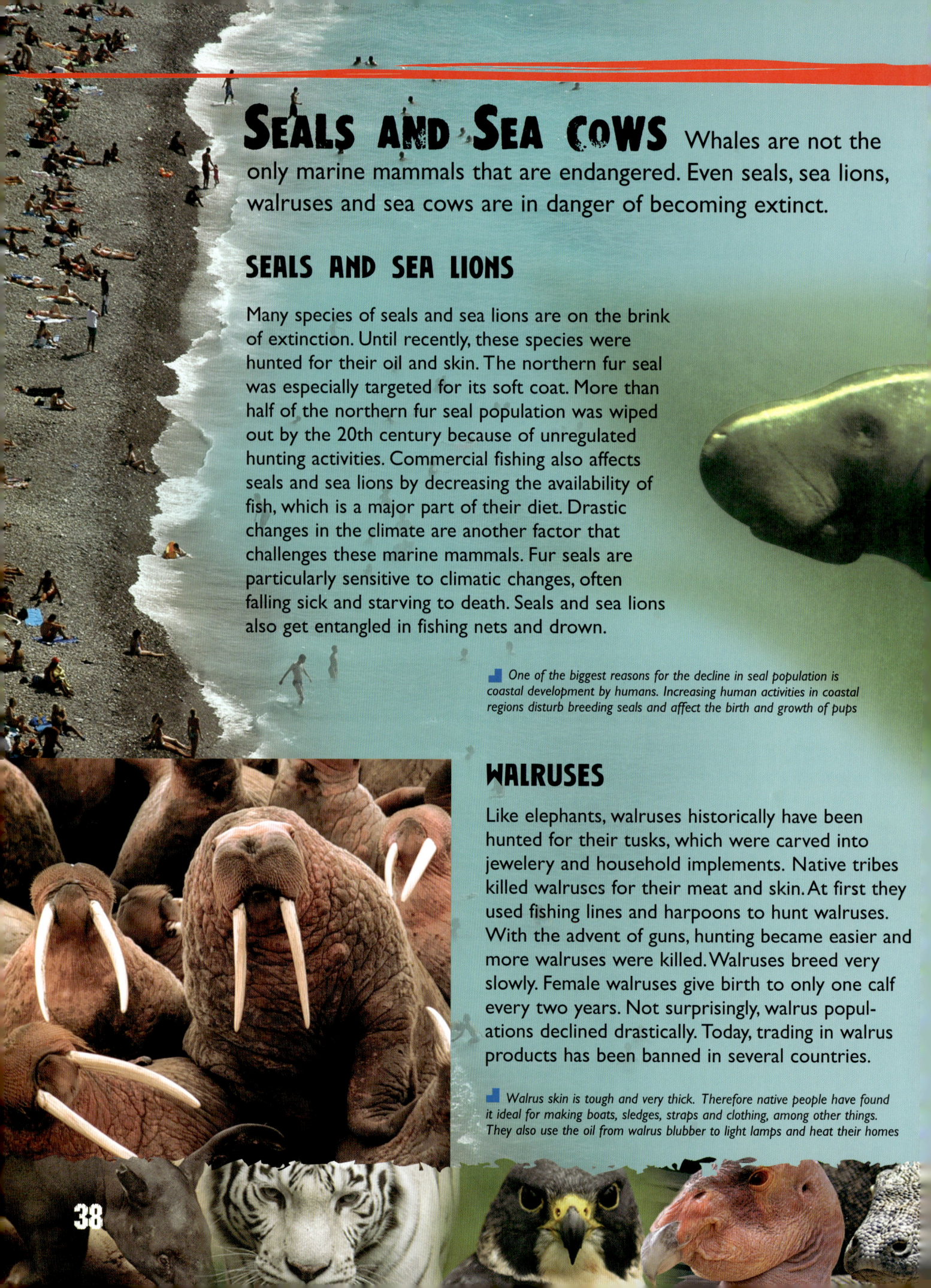

Whales are not the only marine mammals that are endangered. Even seals, sea lions, walruses and sea cows are in danger of becoming extinct.

SEALS AND SEA LIONS

Many species of seals and sea lions are on the brink of extinction. Until recently, these species were hunted for their oil and skin. The northern fur seal was especially targeted for its soft coat. More than half of the northern fur seal population was wiped out by the 20th century because of unregulated hunting activities. Commercial fishing also affects seals and sea lions by decreasing the availability of fish, which is a major part of their diet. Drastic changes in the climate are another factor that challenges these marine mammals. Fur seals are particularly sensitive to climatic changes, often falling sick and starving to death. Seals and sea lions also get entangled in fishing nets and drown.

◾ One of the biggest reasons for the decline in seal population is coastal development by humans. Increasing human activities in coastal regions disturb breeding seals and affect the birth and growth of pups

WALRUSES

Like elephants, walruses historically have been hunted for their tusks, which were carved into jewelery and household implements. Native tribes killed walruses for their meat and skin. At first they used fishing lines and harpoons to hunt walruses. With the advent of guns, hunting became easier and more walruses were killed. Walruses breed very slowly. Female walruses give birth to only one calf every two years. Not surprisingly, walrus populations declined drastically. Today, trading in walrus products has been banned in several countries.

◾ Walrus skin is tough and very thick. Therefore native people have found it ideal for making boats, sledges, straps and clothing, among other things. They also use the oil from walrus blubber to light lamps and heat their homes

ENDANGERED ANIMALS

SEA COWS

Manatees and dugongs are the other marine mammal species that are near extinction. Over many years, humans have hunted both these animals for their hide and meat. In some parts of the Caribbean Islands and South America, the manatee continues to be hunted. Powerboats are another major threat that these animals face. Many manatees and dugongs are killed by collisions with speeding boats. A further reason for the alarming decline in the numbers of these animals is the destruction of the precious seagrass on which they feed.

FACT FILE
ENDANGERED SHARKS

Hawaiian monk seal
Mediterranean monk seal
Caribbean monk seal
Guadalupe fur seal
Northern fur seal
Saimaa seal
Steller sea lion
Manatee
Dugong

▪ *Snorkelling with manatees is a popular tourist attraction in places like Crystal River, in Florida, USA, where they congregate during winter. Divers are advised not to touch, chase, feed or ride manatees, but these instructions are often ignored, disturbing the peaceful existence of the manatees*

EXTINCT SEAL

In 1494 Christopher Columbus was said to have seen *Caribbean monk seals* **on the coast of Santo Domingo. He asked his crew to kill about eight of these animals for food. These seals were then extensively hunted by European sailors and fishers, until the whole species was wiped out. This species was last seen in 1952 off the coast of Seranilla Bank near Jamaica.**

Save the Rodents

Rodents make up more than half of all mammals in the world. They form the largest mammal family and include animals like rats, mice, guinea pigs, beavers, prairie dogs and squirrels. Several rodent species are now either extinct or endangered.

Pest Control

Most rodents are seen as pests. People kill rats and mice as they cause a lot of damage and spread diseases. It is also common for farmers to kill prairie dogs and other burrowing rodents in order to protect their crops. Thousands of burrowing rodents are killed every year with chemicals. Apart from reducing rodent populations, this practice also endangers other animals that may come in contact with the chemicals.

▪ In certain parts of the United States, such as Dakota, farmers use chemicals to control the population of prairie dogs, which are regarded as pests. These regions are also home to one of the most endangered rodents – the black-footed ferret, which preys on prairie dogs. Since the poisoning of prairie dogs directly affects the black-footed ferret, people in these areas have to seek the permission of the conservation authorities before using pesticides

▪ The draining of wetlands surrounding the San Francisco Bay for industrial and housing development has endangered the saltmarsh harvest mouse that is found only in these areas

Habitat Loss

Most rodents like the American harvest mice species, which are found in the wild, are quite harmless, as they do not live too close to human population. However, this scenario is now slowly changing. Humans have cleared many acres of woodlands and forests that were once home to various species of rodents. This has brought the rodents into contact with humans. With no home and not enough food, it is only natural that these rodents enter the houses of people and eat their food and crops.

ENDANGERED ANIMALS

RODENTS FOR SALE!

Some species of rodents, such as chinchillas, have been killed for their soft fur. The chinchilla's fur is believed to be the softest in the world. It is also very dense. It has more than fifty hairs in a single follicle. The fur is so dense that even fleas cannot live on it, as they would suffocate. Millions of chinchillas were killed to make fur coats and stoles. By the end of the 19th century, very few chinchillas were left. Today, a large part of the chinchilla population is kept as pets. Apart from chinchillas, many other rodents are also kept as pets. A large number of rodents, such as guinea pigs, are even used in scientific laboratories for research.

EXTINCT RODENT

Darwin's Galapagos mouse was found only on the island of Santa Cruz. This species thrived in its habitat until the arrival of humans, who brought with them other rodents and animals like black rats, house mice and cats. These animals preyed on the island mice. They also carried diseases that spread quickly and within no time *Darwin's Galapagos mice* became extinct.

▌ The name chinchilla means "little chincha," and has been derived from a South American native tribe called Chincha. The Chinchas lived in the Andes mountains and therefore wore clothes made from chinchilla fur to keep warm

FACT FILE
ENDANGERED RODENT

Asia Minor spiny mouse
Iranian jerboa
Flying squirrel
Short-tailed chinchilla
Shrew rat
Kangaroo rat
Mexican prairie dog
Water rat
Vole
Gopher

Amphibian Alert

Amphibians are animals that spend part of their lives in water and part on land. They include frogs, toads and salamanders. There are over 5000 species of amphibians in the world. Recent studies have revealed that over 3,500 species are endangered, threatened or vulnerable. Of these, more than 400 are critically endangered, the major reason being habitat destruction.

▪ *Destruction of habitat is one of the major reasons for amphibians like the Houston toad becoming endangered*

AMPHIBIAN FOOD

In many countries, especially in Asia, amphibians are an important part of the local diet. In recent years, there has been a steep rise in the demand for frog legs, which are considered a delicacy in most Western countries. In the 1980s, the United States alone imported over 3 million kilograms (6.5 million pounds) of frog meat in a year. Apart from their meat, frogs and toads are also killed for their skin. Wallets and purses made from their skin are sold in countries like Brazil and Thailand. Amphibians are also kept as pets and some species of salamanders are used as bait for fish.

▪ *Excessive killing of frogs for their legs has endangered many frog species. Frog legs are considered a delicacy in countries like France*

POLLUTION

Amphibians are extremely sensitive to climatic changes and even more so to pollution. These animals are some of the worst affected by pollution of air, water and soil. Amphibians also eat insects that often carry harmful chemicals from pesticides. In some developing countries, banned pesticides are still used for better crops. These poisonous chemicals are responsible for the rapid decline in amphibian populations across the world.

▪ *Amphibian eggs are the first to be affected by acid rain that pollutes lakes and streams in which amphibians lay their eggs*

ENDANGERED ANIMALS

ALIEN PREDATORS

The introduction of alien species is also responsible for the decline in amphibian populations in many places. A good example can be found at the Yosemite National Park in the United States. In the 1990s, scientists realized that the population of seven local species of frogs and toads in the National Park had declined. Upon further investigation, they realized that this was probably due to the introduction of trout and bullfrogs into the park. Both trout and bullfrogs not only eat local frogs and their eggs, but also prey on the same insects as the native creatures. This causes a decline in prey populations, and the native species are forced to fight a losing battle against the invaders. Moreover, introduced species also bring with them new diseases that the native population have never known before. The host species itself might be unaffected by the disease as they could have developed an immunity towards it. However, native species are usually vulnerable and the disease can spread, wiping out whole species.

EXTINCT AMPHIBIAN

The *Hula painted frog* inhabited the freshwater wetland of Lake Huleh in Israel. In the 1950s, the swamps in the region were drained to stop the breeding of malarial mosquitoes and to make the land suitable for farming. This led to the extinction of the painted frogs. The last of these frogs was seen in 1955.

FACT FILE
ENDANGERED AMPHIBIANS

MORELET'S TREEFROG
CHINESE GIANT SALAMANDER
VENEZUELAN YELLOW FROG
RANCHO GRANDE HARLEQUIN FROG
GREEN AND RED VENTER HARLEQUIN TOAD
SCARLET HARLEQUIN TOAD
GOLDEN ARROW POISON FROG
GHOST FROG

▌ *The granular salamander is a rare species of salamander found in a small area near Toluca City, Mexico. This critically endangered species breeds in artificial and natural pools in the region. Some species of fish that were introduced into the granular salamander's habitat prey on adult salamanders and the larvae, leading to a drastic decline in their population*

Glossary

Artifact: A tool or decorative showpiece

Blubber: A layer of fat under the skin of marine mammals such as whales and seals

Canine distemper: A highly infectious viral disease of dogs

Captive breeding: Mating a male and female of a species in a controlled environment to produce young ones

Caulk: To seal the cracks between the planks of a boat with waterproof material like tar

Conclude: Decide, or come to an end or decision

Conservation: Protection from harm or loss

Conservationist: Someone who works to protect the environment from destruction or pollution

Decade: A period of ten years

Decline: Reduce in numbers

Deforestation: Cutting down trees

Drastic: Extreme, or severe

Drought: A long period of no rainfall

Dwindling: Reducing, or diminishing

Dysentery: Intestinal infection that causes diarrhea

Ecology: The relationship of living beings with their environment

Encroach: To intrude slowly, or to occupy space beyond one's limits

Enforce: Make sure that certain laws are followed

Estimated: Roughly calculated

Exposed: Laid open to attack or harm

Habitat: The natural home of an animal, bird or plant

Harpoon: An arrow-like weapon attached to a long rope fired from a gun

Illusion: A false impression, or notion

Jeopardy: In danger of being killed or injured

Monitor: Supervise, overlook, or keep track of

Pelt: The skin of a furry animal

Poacher: A person who hunts illegally

Predator: A living being that preys on another living being; any meat-eating animal or bird

Rabies: An infectious viral disease of the nervous system most common in dogs

Raptor: A bird of prey such as an eagle or vulture

Replenish: To put back what has been lost

Rheumatism: A painful disease of the bones

Rodent: The group of animals including rats, mice, squirrels, etc.

Slaughter: Killing, often savage

Souvenir: A memento that reminds someone of a place or event

Stubborn: Unwilling to yield, stubborn

Tagging: Attaching an electronic device to an animal so that scientists can keep track of the particular individual's activities and learn about its lifestyle

Undercoat: The skin that is below an outer coat of fur or skin

Vulnerable: Easily harmed

Index

American alligator 16
Asian elephant 20, 21
Asiatic black bear 26
Black rhinoceros 30, 31
Black-footed ferret 40
Blue whale 34, 35
Bull frogs 43
Bushmeat 10
Cage diving 36
Caimans 16, 17
California condor 8, 23
California gray whale 35
Calipee 18
Canine distemper 33
Canned hunt 28, 29
Chimpanzee 10
Chinchilla 41
Chiru 29
Chum 36
Dhole 32
Dodo 7
Dugong 39
Ethiopian wolf 33
Frog legs 42
Gharials 16, 17

Giant panda 26, 27
Glandular salamander 43
Golden eagle 22
Gorilla 10, 11
Gray wolf 33
Green sea turtle 18
Grevy's zebra 30, 31
Guano 24, 25
Hyacinth macaw 23
Iberian lynx 8
Indian python 18
Indian rhinoceros 30, 31
Java rhinoceros 30, 31
Jellyfish 18
Kakapo 24
Kayapo Indians 23
Kiwi 25
Komodo dragon 18
Lions 7, 14, 15
Manatees 39
Masai warrior 15
Mountain zebra 30, 31
Nile crocodile 16
Ocelot 8
Orangutan 10, 11

Penguins 24, 25
Peregrine falcon 22
Polar bear 26, 27
Prairie dogs 40, 41
Rabies 33
Right whale 34
Salt marsh harvest mouse 40
Sea cows 38, 39
Sea lions 38, 39
Seals 38, 39
Shahtoosh 29
Shark fin soup 36
Sharks 36, 37
Sloth bear 26
Snub-nosed monkey 12
Spix macaw 23
Sumatran rhinoceros 30, 31
Tagging 37
Tapir 30, 31
Tibetan antelope 29
Tigers 15, 32
Turtle soup 18
Walrus 38
Whale oil 34
Whaling 34
White rhinoceros 30, 31
White tiger 14
Wild dogs 32, 33
Wolves 32, 33

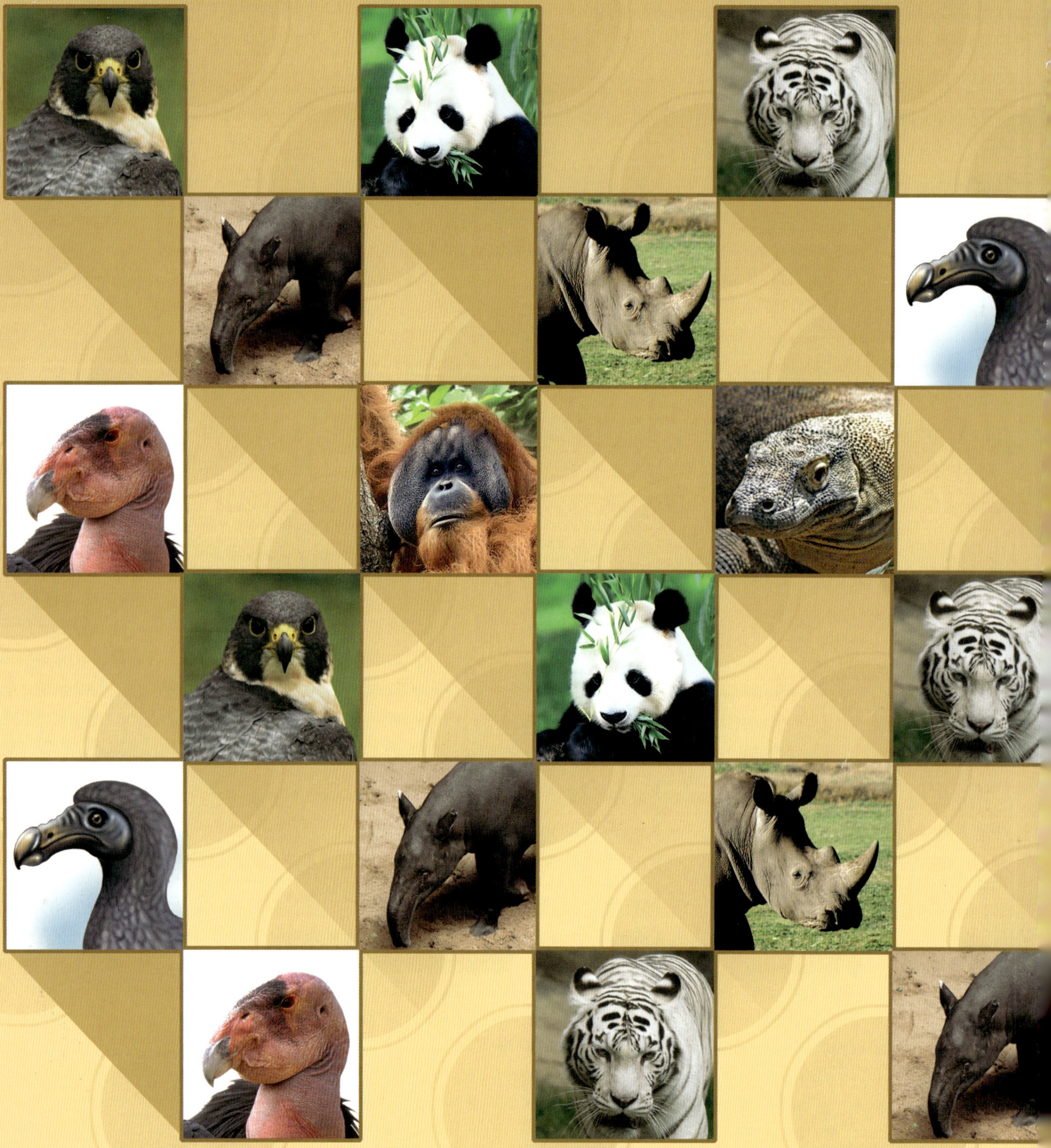